To

A Wonderful
Mum & Dad

NEATH &
PORT TALBOT
REMEMBERED

NEATH &
PORT TALBOT
REMEMBERED

By David Roberts

Courier

breedon **books**
PUBLISHING

First published in Great Britain in 2001 by
The Breedon Books Publishing Company Limited
Breedon House, 3 The Parker Centre, Derby, DE21 4SZ.

ISBN 1 85983 265 2

Printed and bound by Butler & Tanner, Frome, Somerset, England.
Jacket printing by GreenShires, Leicester, England.

Contents

An Appreciation 6

Foreword 7

Introduction 9

Streets of Change 10

Familiar Faces 42

Shopping Spree 62

Early Learning 74

Out of Town 102

Working Ways 126

On the Move 149

Those Special Days 166

What a Performance 184

Team Spirit 195

An Appreciation

This book would not have been possible without the valued assistance of readers of the *Neath & Port Talbot Courier* and the many residents of the two towns who submitted their own images of days gone by. Particular thanks are due to:

John & Pat Killick
Peter & Susan Dargavel
John and Barbara Southward
Peter & the late G.V. Knowles
Phil Owen
Grace Thomas
Bill Adams
Gerrard Lewis
Keith Davies
Robert & Thelma Mason
Jess Crowther
Greville James
Grenfell Morgan
Mr Vernon Joseph
May Lewis
Robert Merrill & Claire Roberts
Neath & Port Talbot Museum & Libraries Service
Cheryl Roberts
John Vivian Hughes
David David
Tony Crocker
Colin Scott and
Steve Powell

Foreword

KEEPING memories alive is an important part of our everyday lives, not just for the present, but for the generations that follow. In an age when change overtakes us quicker than ever, it is all too easy for those memories to fade.

As the 21st century marches on, that is nowhere more evident than within the towns of Neath and Port Talbot. Following on from the success of its companion volumes *Images of Neath & Port Talbot* and *Memory Lane, Neath & Port Talbot,* this book continues a fascinating journey through time.

Its pictorial contents will hold a compelling interest for the casual reader and the historian alike as they revive thoughts of people, places and events. Such an all-embracing mixture of pictures contained within its pages creates a further fitting album to help preserve the past of the two proud towns.

The *Neath & Port Talbot Courier* is delighted to be involved with *Neath & Port Talbot Remembered* and is grateful to all those who made it possible.

George Edwards,
Editorial Director,
Neath & Port Talbot Courier

Introduction

ANYONE returning to Neath and Port Talbot after even a few years absence could be forgiven for their surprise at what awaits them. For where once decades passed with only minimal disruption, change can now occur far quicker. There is much evidence of this in both towns.

As neighbours, they have grown up together and though there are many similarities in their everyday lives each retains its own distinct identity.

Mainly because of their geographical position both towns were thrown into the cauldron of change that was the industrial revolution. If Wales was the world's first nation to be fully taken in its grip, then Neath and Port Talbot were in its vanguard and still bear many scars to prove it.

Rural settlements were overtaken by the building of works and the sinking of mines. Coal, copper, iron, steel and tinplate all played their part in the transformation that followed. The industries and their machines needed new transport links and men; men – and their families – needed housing. Added together the result was rapid change.

Time has taken everything full circle. The heavy industry has faded. Slower perhaps than the speed with which it was born, but with just as devastating an effect. What once created jobs now creates unemployment.

Today, Neath and Port Talbot are united as a County Borough and face the fight for 21st century survival together. That means more changes as new, Hi-Tech industries and their state-of-the-art production methods fill the gap left by the departure of the old.

Much of what has happened has been well-documented, but the images in this pictorial compilation play a complementary role and colour the picture of a fascinating past. People, places and events all play their part.

Spanning three centuries, *Neath & Port Talbot Remembered* tells it as it was.

David Roberts
Summer 2001

Streets of Change

High Street, Aberavon, late 1890s, and an obliging crowd gathers for the photographer.

Penywern Road, Neath, 1890s. Now it is the main route from the town towards Pontardawe.

A view from Pentyla over Vivian Square, Aberavon, early 1900s.

This was the Gnoll School, Gnoll Park Road, Neath, in 1908. The site is now occupied by the divisional police headquarters.

High Street, Aberavon, looking eastwards, 1905.

Windsor Road, Neath, looking towards the town's railway station around 1900.

Looking down Station Road, Port Talbot, towards the Grand Hotel, 1907.

Briton Ferry Road, Neath, 1905. Stockham's roundabout was later constructed here.

Water Street, Aberavon, 1909.

Orchard Street, Neath, viewed from Victoria Gardens, 1909.

High Street, Aberavon, 1910.

The Commercial Hotel, at the junction of Windsor Road and Alfred Street, Neath, 1910. It later became the Cambrian Hotel and then The Station House.

The view over Aberavon from Mynydd Dinas, in 1920. St Mary's Church can be seen dominating the surrounding houses.

Eastland Road, Neath, looking towards the Drill Hall, 1905.

Penycae, Port Talbot, mid-1920s.

Victoria Gardens and St David's Road, Neath, early 1920s. The Gnoll House can be seen in the top left of the picture.

Lower Water Street, Aberavon, late 1920s.

An aerial view of Neath, 1929. The buildings below the railway line have long since disappeared.

A mountainside view of Port Talbot dominated by the Talbot Athletic Ground, late 1920s. The town's steelworks is in the background and the railway line curving out of the bottom left ran to Dyffryn locomotive sheds.

Victoria Gardens bus station, Neath, with St David's Church behind, 1932.

Aberavon railway station, 1928. The nearby crossing gates were the source of much traffic congestion and resulted in the building – during the mid-1960s – of the M4 Port Talbot by-pass.

Green Street, Neath, showing one of the market entrances, 1934.

A late 1940s view along Station Road, Port Talbot, from its notorious level crossing traffic bottleneck.

Windsor Road, Neath, 1938, showing the town's former police station with court rooms behind.

The Odeon Cinema, Bethany Square, Port Talbot, overshadows this Maesteg-bound, Llynfi Motors bus, waiting – with its conductress – near the Station Road pedestrian crossing, mid-1950s.

Library Road, Neath, looking towards Cimla, late 1940s.

A passing train delays traffic at the level crossing in Station Road, Port Talbot, 1958.

Gnoll Avenue, Neath, 1949.

Torrential rain brought heavy flooding to Talbot Road, Port Talbot, in 1960. The Plaza cinema is on the left.

Passengers wait to board a bus at The Parade, Neath, 1950.

High Street, Aberavon, 1969. Before long its buildings would be demolished to make way for town centre redevelopment.

Windsor Road, Neath, viewed from Stockham's roundabout in 1951. The building of the town's southern link road brought the demolition of many of the houses, in the early 1970s.

Water Street Back Lane, Port Talbot, looking towards the town's Municipal Buildings, 1969.

Demolition, to make way for town centre redevelopment, takes its toll on High Street, Aberavon, 1969.

Orchard Street, Neath, early 1952. Woolworth's store is here today.

Orchard Street, Neath, May 1952.

The Railway Tavern, Lower Water Street, Aberavon, 1970.

The bandstand at Victoria Gardens, Neath, decorated in celebration of the Coronation of Queen Elizabeth II, June 1953.

Lloyd's Bank, High Street, Aberavon, retains a solitary link with the past as the Aberafan Shopping Centre takes shape, behind, in the early 1970s.

Bridge Street, Neath, during reconstruction of Neath river bridge, 1958.

A view along Bridge Street, Neath, into the town, September 1958.

Looking down Port Talbot's bottle-neck Water Street, 1970.

Once Port Talbot had two Woolworth stores. This one, in Church Street, opposite the Municipal Buildings, pictured in 1970, was often referred to as the old one. The newer Woolworth store at the time was in Station Road.

Orchard Street, Neath, looking towards Victoria Gardens, 1958.

Looking across the High Street bridge over the River Afan, Port Talbot, 1970.

Orchard Street, Neath, and the Gwyn Hall, 1959.

Work on Port Talbot town centre's, River Afan flood defence walls, late 1970s.

Windsor Road, Neath, near the town's railway station approach, late 1950s.

Penydre, Neath looking towards the town centre, January 1959. The Star Inn is on the left.

The Parade, Neath, 1960.

Pedestrianisation was decades away when this 1965 picture of New Street, Neath, looking towards Victoria Gardens was taken.

One of the open-top, double-deck buses used in summer on Thomas Bros' services to and from Aberavon Beach heads back into Port Talbot along Victoria Road, 1970.

The Three Cranes pub, Wind Street, Neath, mid-1960s.

London Road, Neath, looking towards Stockham's roundabout, 1971.

Port Talbot's General Post Office, Station Road, 1972.

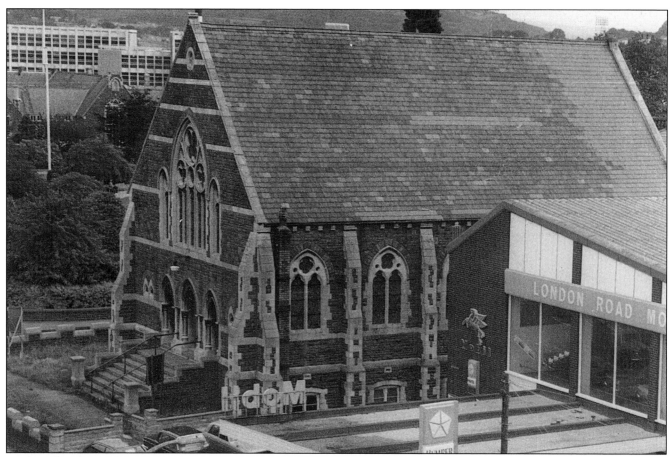

Wesley Church, London Road, Neath, 1974. It was later demolished and replaced by sheltered housing accommodation and a doctors' surgery.

A heavy overnight snowfall in February 1978 left Bethany Square – and much of the rest of Port Talbot – empty of traffic.

The M4 at Pentyla, Port Talbot, almost empty of traffic after the heavy snowfall of February 1978.

Great Western Chambers and The Croft, Neath, 1974.

Queen Street, Port Talbot, 1988. It was later demolished to make way for the town's Tesco supermarket.

Water Street, Neath, looking towards Old Market Street, during building of the town's second Tesco store and multi-storey car park, 1977.

The Majestic Bingo Hall, Forge Road, Port Talbot, in 1988. Originally the Majestic, and then Odeon cinemas, it was later demolished to make way for redevelopment of the town's shopping area.

Water Street, Neath, looking towards Victoria Gardens, November 1977.

Familiar Faces

The Jones family of Tonmawr, about 1900. Industrialists, they were involved in the operation of small mines in the area. William Jones was a councillor, Justice of the Peace and chairman of Neath Rural District Council.

Neath stage and screen star of the 1930s and 1940s, Maudie Edwards, with her husband, family and friends, all set to leave Neath railway station on the first leg of a journey to the United States, 1936.

Deacons of Ebenezer Chapel, Port Talbot, 1911.

A group of residents from Melyncrythan, Neath, on a charabanc outing to Porthcawl, 1929.

Staff of the Victoria Road, Aberavon, branch of the Taibach and Port Talbot Co-operative Society, on a trip to Blackpool, 1931.

Messing about in boats was great fun for these lads on a vessel moored near the mouth of the River Afan, in the late 1940s.

Members of a Neath choir take a break from rehearsals, July 1938.

Members of Cwmavon YWCA on a holiday trip, 1948.

Regulars of the Apple Tree pub, Elias Street, Neath, on an outing in the late 1940s.

Members of Trefelin Workingmen's Club, Velindre, Port Talbot, on a night out, 1948.

Members of Windsor Square Methodist Church, Stockham's Corner, Neath, take a break from decorating the building, 1948.

The West End Gang. Three likely lads from Taibach, Port Talbot, after a hard day's adventure around the Ffrydwyllt tinplate works, 1949.

Members of the congregation of London Road Methodist Church, Neath, late 1940s.

Parents and children of the congregation of Rock Chapel, Cwmavon, during their Christmas party, 1950.

Neath star Maudie Edwards surrounded by old friends during a return to her former school at Melyncrythan, in the mid-1950s.

The oldest residents of Marsh Street, Aberavon, toast Queen Elizabeth II on her Coronation, during a celebration street party,
June 1953.

This gathering outside Dyfed Road Health Clinic, Neath, in 1947 was unique. All the mums in the picture had given birth to twins.

Members of Trefelin Workingmen's Club, Port Talbot, with their families and friends on a trip to Porthcawl, 1954.

Employees of Marks and Spencer's Neath store at their annual dance at the Castle Hotel, 1950.

The Golf Road gang, Sandfields, Port Talbot, 1955.

Members of the 1st Neath Guides and Greenwoods at Neath Methodist Church, Stockham's Corner, 1952.

A group of worshipers from All Saint's Church, Cwmavon, at the nearby rugby ground after taking part in the annual Whitsun procession through the village, 1952. The now-demolished church can be seen in the background.

A group of residents from
Brynbryddan, Cwmavon, all set
for a day out, 1957.

Two young friends take a break
from their playtime in Pendrill
Street, Neath, 1953.

Members of Trefelin Workingmen's Club, Velindre, Port Talbot, enjoy a pint, 1959.

Cimla Sunday School children outside the Welfare Hall, Cimla, Neath, 1955.

Men from the reclamation department of the Steel Company of Wales, Port Talbot, on a night out at Mumbles, early 1960s.

Guests at a Neath Post Office staff party, 1955.

Staff and friends at a retirement party for the foreman of Smart's Bakery, Port Talbot, 1967.

Staff of Phillips Brothers Outfitters, Neath, on an outing to Tenby, 1956.

Members of Cwmavon Boys Club, 1976.

Residents of Shelone Road, Briton Ferry, 1957.

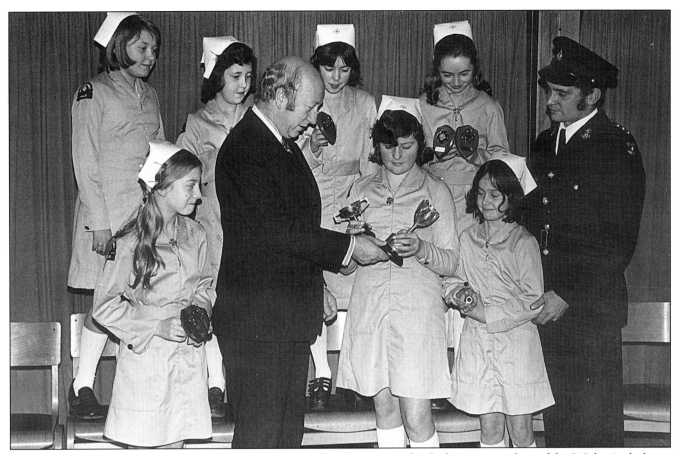

The presentation of first aid competition awards to pupils of Bryn Primary School who were members of the St John Ambulance Brigade, by headteacher Gerrard Lewis, late 1970s.

Some of the 300 children who attended the Briton Ferry and Neath Co-operative Society's annual children's Christmas party at St Catherine's church hall, Melyncrythan, 1958.

Film star Elizabeth Taylor at Pontrhydyfen with the family of Richard Burton shortly after his death in 1984.

Members of the 3rd Neath Scouts, with their leaders, 1960.

Manning the stalls at Pontrhydyfen Primary School's summer fete, 1982.

Mayor, Alderman T E C Molland, inspects some of the blooms at Neath Horticultural Society's annual show, November 1962.

Neath's twin mayoresses, Grace and Katherine Molland, at a jumble sale at St David's church hall, Neath, 1963.

A group of Neath teenagers at Neath railway station before leaving for an exchange visit to Holland, 1968.

Friends and colleagues of newly-installed Mayor of the Borough of Afan, Ted Owen, gather to celebrate, 1976.

Members of the congregation of Neath Wesleyan Church, London Road, celebrate Wesley Day, 1969.

Shopping Spree

For complete house furnishing, J. Kahn, of Westgate House, High Street, Port Talbot, was the place to go in the 1890s.

Stockham's bakery, Windsor Road, Neath, early 1900s.

T. Nicholas & Sons, tea and provisions merchants, was just one of the stores that helped make Station Road the place to shop in Port Talbot, early 1900s.

The India and China Tea Company, Water Street, Aberavon, 1905. Later it became the Home & Colonial store.

G. Oliver's boot and shoe store, Green Street, Neath, 1905.

The ironmongery store, with an array of hardware displayed outside, at Melyncrythan, Neath, 1908.

Allins, bakers and provision merchants, Wind Street, Neath, 1910.

Williams Cloth Hall outfitters, Water Street, Aberavon, 1906.

Boots store, Water Street, Aberavon, 1913.

Lewis's tailors and outfitters, Villiers Street, Briton Ferry, 1920.

Griffiths & Sons, gents outfitters, Station Road, Port Talbot, about 1910.

Halfords, Green Street, Neath in the mid-1950s. Staff are seen trying to stem the flow of flood water that engulfed parts of the town after torrential rain.

H.W. Keey, jewellers, Talbot Square, Aberavon, about 1910.

Lennards shoe shop dominates a corner of the junction of Orchard Street and Green Street, Neath, early 1950s.

A family gathering outside McFadyen's shop, 41 Victoria Road, Aberavon, 1933.

Staff and customers of Port Talbot butcher Jock Martin, High Street, Aberavon, early 1960s.

This little girl poses across the road from Nellie Rees's sweet shop, St David's Road, Neath, early 1950s.

Water Street, Aberavon, showing the David Evans store and, alongside Cavendish furnishers and Elizabeth Player children's clothing stores, 1967.

Green Street, Neath, showing Marks & Spencer, mid-1960s.

High Street, Aberavon, showing the Angel Hotel and John M. Smith, ironmongers, 1967.

Jim Morgan & Sons motorcycle dealers, Windsor Road, Neath, 1971.

Woolworths, Church Street, Aberavon, store and the Civic electrical store, 1967.

Bert Veale's music store, New Street, Neath, mid-1970s.

Dewhurst the butchers, Wind Street, Neath, and alongside, The Three Cranes public house, late 1980s.

J. Coles, young man's clothing shop, Evans pie shop and Eddie Thomas's shoe repair shop, Water Street, Aberavon, 1968.

Loyds electrical store, Wind Street, Neath, early 1970s.

Early Learning

Class 3A Melyn Girls' School, Neath, 1911.

Standard 4 Aberavon Church of England Boys' School, 1922.

Briton Ferry schoolchildren dressed as children from many nations, 1912.

Boys of Eastern School, Taibach, Port Talbot, with their teacher, at Ogmore school camp, January 1950.

Standard 3B, Gnoll Senior Girls' School, Neath, 1920.

Pupils of Cwmavon Junior School, Port Talbot, 30 April 1954.

Cwrt Sart Central School, Briton Ferry, 1928.

Mountain Infants School, Aberavon, 1955.

Class 1, Neath Road Infants School, Briton Ferry, 1930.

St Joseph's Primary School, Aberavon, 1955.

The percussion band at Herbert Road Junior School, Melyncrythan, Neath, 1931.

Tywyn Infants School, Sandfields, Port Talbot, 1955.

Llansawel Primary School, Briton Ferry, 1933.

Swimming lessons for children from Cwmavon Junior School – at Morfa Beach – 1956.

Brynhyfryd Girls' Junior School, Briton Ferry, 1936.

An art class at Eastern Boys Primary School, Taibach, Port Talbot, 1956.

Gnoll Road Congregational Church Sunday School, Neath, 1936.

Tirmorfa Junior School, Sandfields, Port Talbot, 1958.

Neath Boys' Grammar School, 1948.

Mountain Boys' School, Aberavon, 1958.

Girls from Gnoll Secondary School, Neath, at Ogmore school camp, 1949.

Tywyn Infants School, Sandfields, Port Talbot, 1959.

Boys from Neath Grammar School on a trip to Stratford-upon-Avon, May 1, 1949.

Cwmavon Junior School, Port Talbot, 1959.

Form 5B, Neath Boys' Grammar School, 1950.

Baglan Infants School, Port Talbot, early 1960s.

Standard 4, Alderman Davies' Church-in-Wales School, Neath, 1956.

Baglan Infants School, Port Talbot, early 1960s.

Melyncrythan Junior Girls' School, Neath, 1956.

Cwrt Sart Junior School, spring 1961 – after the 11-plus.

Form 5Q, Neath Boys' Grammar School, 1961.

Trefelin Secondary Modern School, Velindre, Port Talbot, 1959.

Llansawel Primary School, Briton Ferry, 1963.

Class 5B, Gnoll Primary School, Neath, mid-1960s.

Cwmavon Primary School Nursery Class, Port Talbot, 1962.

Alderman Davies' Church-in-Wales Girls' School, Neath, 1967.

Prefects of Sandfields Comprehensive School, Port Talbot, 1964.

Gnoll Infants School, Neath, 1968.

Class 4, Glyncorrwg Junior School, Port Talbot, 1966.

Cwmavon Junior School, Port Talbot, 1966.

Brynhyfryd Primary School, Briton Ferry, 1968.

The late Lord Heycock hands over an award at Cymmer Afan Youth Wing's first annual presentation evening, in the early 1970s.

Pontrhydyfen Welsh Primary School, 1975.

Bryn Primary School, Port Talbot, early 1970s.

Class 3, Alderman Davies' Church-in-Wales School, Neath, 1979.

Glanymor Infants School, Sandfields, Port Talbot, 1974.

Children of Groes Primary School, Margam, pay a visit to the Mayor of Port Talbot, Alderman James Warren, 1974.

Alderman Davies' Church-in-Wales School, Neath, June 1980.

St David's Day at Central Infants
School, Port Talbot, 1978.

Gnoll Infants School, Neath, 1980.

Nursery and infant pupils at Blaen Baglan School, Port Talbot, St David's Day, 1980.

Form 4N, Dyffryn Comprehensive School, Margam, Port Talbot, 1980.

Class 4D, Alderman Davies' Church-in-Wales School, Neath, 1965.

Sandfields Comprehensive School, Port Talbot, 1981.

Pupils of Crynallt Infants School, Cimla, Neath, celebrate St David's Day, 1985.

Bryn Primary School, Port Talbot, 1983.

St David's Day celebrations at Crynallt Infants School, Cimla, Neath, 1986.

Form 3I, Glanafan Comprehensive Lower School, Port Talbot, 1983.

Out of Town

Cwmavon, showing All Saints' Church in the early 1900s.

Church Road, Cadoxton, Neath, early 1900s.

The newly-laid road from Aberavon to the beach, early 1900s.

Tabernacle Street, Skewen, 1904.

Aberavon Beach, early 1900s.

Grandison Street, Briton Ferry, 1905.

A view of Cwmavon, early 1900s.

The shoe repairers at Seven Sisters, 1910.

An impressive ornamental fountain at Margam Park, Port Talbot, 1904.

The primary school and Soar Chapel, Seven Sisters, 1910.

Groes village and Beulah Chapel – the Round Chapel – Margam, 1905.

Villiers Street, Briton Ferry, 1910.

Baglan House, Baglan, 1913.

High Street, Taibach, 1905.

The old chapel, Pen Pentre, Crynant, 1910.

Ynysdfan Bridge, Cwmavon, 1918.

Looking down the Afan Valley, across Ynysygwas, Cwmavon, early 1920s.

An aerial view of Taibach, Port Talbot, showing the Memorial Park, 1929.

Penrhiwtyn House, Melyncrythan, Neath, 1910.

The promenade at Aberavon Beach, overlooked by the Jersey Beach Hotel, early 1920s.

The reservoir on the Jersey Estate, Briton Ferry, 1911.

Tymaen, Cwmavon, late 1920s.

Commercial Road, Resolven, 1914.

The entrance to the Ladies Walk, Baglan, at the top end of what became Thorney Road, late 1940s.

Cwrt Sart School, Briton Ferry. It was originally a nurses' home and annexe to the Third Western Military Hospital – now Neath General Hospital – during World War One.

Neath Abbey, mid-1920s.

Victoria Road, Aberavon, 1947.

A view of Briton Ferry from the top end of Ynysmaerdy Road, 1921.

Brynbryddan, Cwmavon, mid-1950s.

The Great pond at the Gnoll Grounds, Neath, 1922.

St Catharine's Church, Baglan, early 1950s.

High Street, Glynneath, at the crossroads, near the Dinas Rock Hotel, early 1930s.

Railway bridges dominated the lower end of Villiers Street, Briton Ferry, when this picture was taken in the mid-1930s.

A view of Cwmavon from the Bwlch Mountain, 1955.

Abbey Road, Neath and the banana island, as it is known, late 1940s.

The promenade at Aberavon Beach, 1956.

Neath Road, Briton Ferry, near its junction with Old Road, Baglan, in the late 1940s. The buildings were later demolished to make way for Briton Ferry roundabout.

The sunken gardens at Aberavon Beach, 1963.

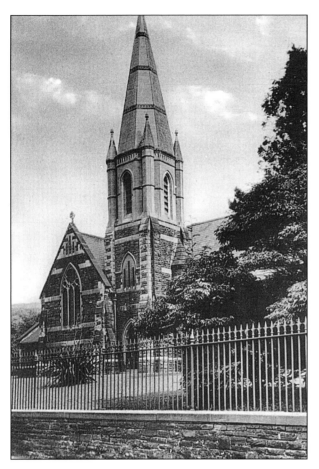

A back lane view of Bryn, dominated by the village's huge colliery tip, in the mid-1960s.

St Anne's Church, Tonna, late 1940s.

Dwr-y-Felin Road, Neath, 1952.

The eastern end of Aberavon Beach, dominated by the Miami Beach Amusement Park and its figure-of-eight ride, mid-1960s.

The rose garden, Jersey Park, Briton Ferry, 1956. The rest shelter was burned down by vandals early in 2001.

Briton Ferry Public Hall, pictured in 1958.

Drainage work during the tip reclamation scheme, Bryn, Port Talbot, May 1975.

Building of the access road above Cimla Common, Neath, 1968.

A view of Glyncorrwg, Afan Valley, 1968.

Earth moving machines at work re-contouring Bryn colliery tip, Port Talbot, 1977.

A huge forestry fire which swept across the mountain at Pontrhydyfen threatened to engulf houses at Efail Fach, 1982.

Working Ways

Workmen at the Copper Miners Tinplate Works, Cwmavon, pictured alongside the Pelton wheel assembly that helped provide its power, early 1900s.

Workmen lay tramlines along Neath Road, Briton Ferry, late 1890s.

Workers at the Burrows Works, Water Street, Aberavon, 1900.

Men and women tinplate workers – openers, benders and throwers – at Mansel Tinplate Works, Port Talbot, 1900.

Laundry workers at the Third Western Military Hospital, later Neath General Hospital, 1916.

Cwmavon tinplate workers, 1918.

The Empress Tinplate Works, Cwmavon, 1910.

A group of Port Talbot workmen employed on laying the new road from Cwmavon to Maesteg, 1925.

The Eaglesbush Tinplate Works, Melyncrythan, Neath, 1917.

Workmen engaged on laying the Ynys playing fields, Velindre, in the early 1920s.

Young women from the Japan Works, Melyncrythan, Neath, all dressed up for the photographer, 1919.

Colliers at Glenavon Top Level, Cymmer, 1927.

The Mines Rescue team at Blaenant colliery in the Dulais Valley, mid-1920s.

An aerial view of Briton Ferry steelworks and the dock looking up river towards Neath, July 1934.

The station master and staff, Aberavon railway station, about 1920.

A group of Neath railwaymen, 1936.

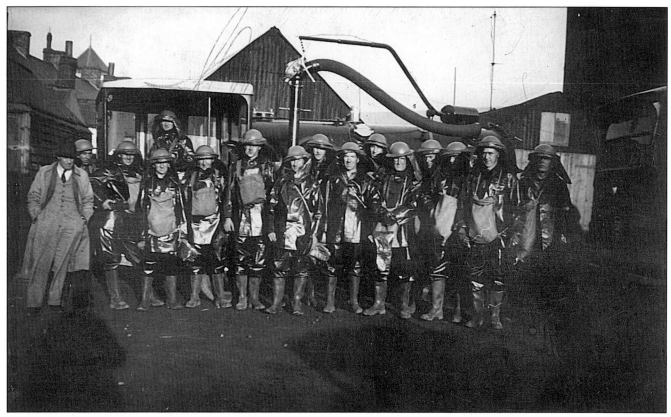

Council workmen at Burrows Yard, Water Street, Aberavon, on World War Two Air Raid Precautions duty, 1940.

Post Office bicycle telegraph messengers in a spot of high jinks at Neath railway station yard, 1937.

Construction of the Abbey Works, Port Talbot, late 1949.

A group of Air Raid Precaution wardens – and their dog – at Neath, 1941.

Aberavon midwife Boppa John who served the community from the 1920s through to the 1950s.

Staff of Victoria Road, Co-operative store, Aberavon, 1941.

Miners waiting to enter the cage to descend to the pit bottom at Cefn Coed Colliery, Crynant, 1947. It is likely that they were pictured on January 1, and were part of the first shift there after nationalisation of the coal industry that day.

Staff of Neath Galvanising Works, 1948.

Employees of Marks and Spencer, Green Street, Neath, 1950.

Colleagues of Wyn Mills gather at a ceremony to mark his retirement after 45 years as a Port Talbot steelworker, April 17, 1949.

Nursing staff at Port Talbot General Hospital, 1950.

Arthur the Oil, as he was known, with his horse and cart in Wellfield Avenue, Neath, 1952. The lucky children had a ride on his cart, the others simply trailed behind.

Mechanics and staff in the workshop of the Talbot Road, Port Talbot, garage of motor dealer Oscar Chess, in the early 1950s.

British Rail office staff at Neath, 1952.

Construction work on Briton Ferry viaduct, late 1953.

Hugh Gaitskill, Chancellor of the Exchequer, officially opens the Steel Company of Wales Port Talbot plant, July 1951.

Barmaids Mary Jones and Bessie Carpenter at their post in the saloon bar of the Cambrian Hotel, Windsor Road, Neath, 1956.

Teaching staff of Eastern Secondary School, Taibach, Port Talbot, 1955.

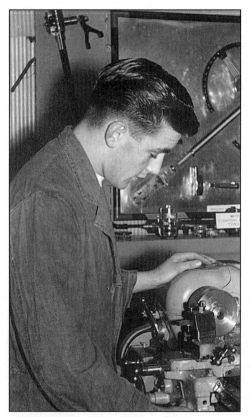

Staff of Shufflebothams china store and warehouse, Neath, 1960.

An apprentice uses a lathe at the Resolven, Neath, works of George Kent, later Cam Gears and TRW steering systems, 1957.

Trainee blast furnace foremen at the Steel Company of Wales, Port Talbot Works, 1958.

Teaching staff at Ynysymaerdy Primary School, Briton Ferry, 1962.

Duffryn Rhondda Colliery, Afan Valley, Port Talbot, 1958.

Staff of the South Wales Electricity Board's Neath office, 1963.

The Port Talbot Docks diver and his crew, 1965.

Engineering workers at Port Talbot Docks, 1968.

Bottling of Calor gas at Llandarcy refinery, Neath, 1965.

Staff of Macfisheries, Station Road, Port Talbot, 1969.

Employees of Woolworth's Neath store, early 1970s.

Tobacco leaf stripping at the Port Talbot factory of cigar makers JR Freeman and Son, 1970.

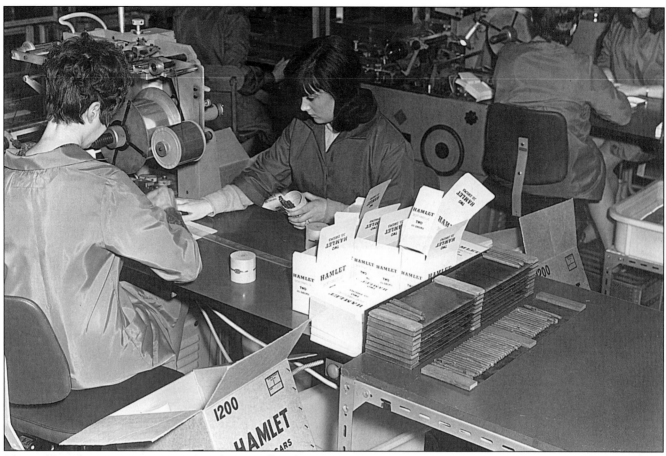

The packing plant at JR Freeman and Son's Port Talbot factory, 1970.

Teaching staff at Groes Primary School, Port Talbot, 1972. The building was soon to vanish under the advancing M4.

On the Move

The driver of a horse-drawn Hansom cab, waits for a fare at Neath railway station, late 1890s.

Sailing vessels laid up at Llewellyn's Quay, Port Talbot Docks, 1895.

Briton Ferry Dock, 1915.

This was how bakers and confectioners HB Comley & Sons Ltd, of Station Road, Port Talbot, made their deliveries in 1905.

A hansom cab, provided for guests of the Walnut Tree Hotel, High Street, Port Talbot, pictured between Port Talbot's railway station and the Grand Hotel, 1907.

Staff of George Phillips, fruiterers, Neath, with the company's second lorry, at Briton Ferry, mid-1920s.

The wreck of the *Amazon*, on the sands at Taibach, 1 September 1908.

One of the Richmond company's buses that ferried passengers around Neath, 1920s.

Port Talbot Docks, mid-1920s.

This van was used by Heard's, wholesale confectioners, in Neath, 1948.

Port Talbot railway station, late 1920s.

The Trebor sweets advertisement was a familiar sight around Neath in the early 1950s, on the side of this van operated by wholesale confectioners, Heard's.

An aerial view of the mouth of the River Afan, and the entrance to Port Talbot Docks, 1929.

The locomotive sheds, originally used by the Neath and Brecon Railway, at Neath Riverside station, early 1950s.

The railway station at Bryn, Port Talbot, late 1940s.

Electrically-powered delivery vans of the Taibach and Port Talbot Co-operative Society, mid-1950s.

A 1956 view of Neath Riverside station showing a train on the high level, Swansea to Paddington, line crossing overhead.

This Sandfields resident was only too happy to pose for the photographer on his new BSA motorcycle, in 1958.

Dr Edwards, of Cwmavon, and railway signalman Jack Rees, with the doctor's Daimler car, late 1950s.

Neath railway station, 1956. The train at the platform was an enthusiasts' special organised by Gloucestershire Railway Society.

Aberavon railway station, 1959.

A train waits at Resolven station, mid-1950s.

These Leyland Tiger Cub buses ferried countless passengers around Port Talbot for Thomas Bros. This picture was taken in Talbot Road, mid-1960s.

A civic send-off for the first meals-on-wheels delivery undertaken by the Neath branch of the Women's Voluntary Service in its new Austin Mini van, 1962. The mayor was Alderman T E C Molland.

If you needed ferrying around Port Talbot Docks in 1965 then the Avon was the vessel to do the job.

The Briton Ferry depot of the N&C Luxury Coach company, mid-1960s.

The Port Talbot Docks pilot vessel, Margam Abbey, 1965.

Passengers prepare to board a Creamline service bus at Afan Valley Road, Cimla, Neath, late 1960s.

One of the open-topped, double decker buses operated by Thomas Bros, of Port Talbot, on routes to and from Aberavon Beach, leaving the firm's Acacia Avenue, Sandfields garage, mid-1960s.

A flotilla of pleasure craft moored near the mouth of the River Afan, 1978.

This Creamline Services double decker careered off the road at Pontrhydyfen, while carrying passengers to a Swansea supermarket, on October 9, 1986.

The Port Talbot docks pilot vessel, Margam Abbey, 1983.

Some of the milestones in and around Neath and Port Talbot that told travellers in early times where they were and how far they had to go to reach their destination. Each of these mileage markers survives to this day.

Those Special Days

Baptist churchgoers gather for the annual Whitsun procession through Neath, 1905.

Aberavon Scouts on parade alongside St Theodore's Church, Port Talbot, 1910.

A funeral procession makes its way past the tram depot in London Road, Neath, 1910. Tom Evans of undertakers John Evans and Sons, Melyncrythan, is seated alongside the coachman. The tram depot is now a tyre fitting centre.

Members of Ebenezer Church pass along High Street, Aberavon, during their Whitsun procession, 1911.

Neath couple Frank Pickering and Vi Lane at their wedding in 1921.

An Aberavon wedding group, 1920s.

Mr Tom Phillips and his bride Fanny Pickering with attendants at their 1924, Neath wedding.

These youngsters from the Cottage Homes, Bryncoch, Neath, would certainly have remembered the day they had their picture taken with civic dignitaries outside the town's Gwyn Hall, 1926.

A 1920s Port Talbot wedding group.

Neighbours of Florence Street, Neath, celebrate the Coronation of King George VI, 1937.

The first Baptism of Cwmavon gospel Mission at Ynysafan bridge, 31 May 1924.

Mounted police head the annual mayoral procession through the streets of Neath, 1939.

The congregation gathers for the closing of Rock Chapel, Pwllyglaw, Cwmavon, 1931.

Residents of Green Park, Aberavon, at their VE Day party, 1945.

Girl Guides marching in Neath's annual civic parade, 1939.

A bride and groom with attendants after their Neath wedding, 1948.

Youngsters from Wesleyan Methodist Church take part in the annual Whitsun procession at Cwmavon, 1952.

St David's Church choir boys walk along Windsor Road, Neath, during a civic procession, late 1950s.

Residents of Lingfield Avenue, Sandfields, Port Talbot, at their street party to mark the Coronation of Queen Elizabeth II, 1953.

Fancy dress was the order of the day for these residents of Florence Street, Neath, when they celebrated the Festival of Britain, August 1951.

Youngsters of Warren Place, Aberavon, during celebrations to mark the Coronation of Queen Elizabeth II, 1953.

Pendrill Street, Neath, Carnival Queen and attendants, 1951.

An Aberavon wedding group, 1954.

Youngsters from St David's Church, Neath, during the town's 1953 Whitsun procession.

Traffic was brought to a halt in Port Talbot on June 9, 1958 for the funeral of Leading Fireman Wilfrid Humphry Mogford. More than 50 of his colleagues lined the route when a fire tender carried the coffin from his home at Fairfield, Aberavon, to St Theodore's Church and later the Chapel of Ease cemetery.

Youngsters in Pendrill Street, Neath, prepare to take part in a carnival parade, 1953.

Residents of Gwendoline Street, Port Talbot, in fancy dress to commemorate the Investiture of the Prince of Wales, 1969.

Members of the congregation of London Road Methodist Church prepare to set off on Neath's 1953 Whitsun procession.

Children from Gwendoline Street, Port Talbot, at their street party tea to mark the Investiture of the Prince of Wales, 1969.

Youngsters from Bethel Street, Briton Ferry, dressed up for the Whitsun procession at Briton Ferry, 1960.

Neighbours of Trefelin Street, Velindre, Port Talbot, during celebrations to mark the Investiture of the Prince of Wales, 1969.

Mayor of Neath in 1962-63, Alderman T E C Molland, with the impressive mayoral chain, during a civic event at Glynneath.

Neath's 1962 Mayoral year was a unique occasion. The Mayor, Alderman T E C Molland chose both his twin daughters, Grace and Kathryn as mayoresses. One officiated for the first six months of his year of office, the other for the remaining period.

Crowds gather to watch a Christmas parade – complete with Chinese dragon – at Station Road, Port Talbot, early 1980s.

Civic dignitaries attend the annual wreath laying ceremony at Briton Ferry war memorial, alongside Neath Road, November 1962.

These youngsters at Pontrhydyfen take a break from celebrations to mark the wedding of Prince Charles and Lady Diana Spencer, July 29, 1981.

Residents of Grove Road, Curtis Street and Jenkins Road, Neath, united to celebrate the Investiture of the Prince of Wales, 1969.

What a Performance

Neath Orpheus Male Voice Society, November 1915.

Port Talbot and District Workmen's Prize Band, again with its three young recruits, early 1920s.

A member of Port Talbot and District Workmen's Prize Band, with three young, but keen, recruits, early 1920s.

Neath stage and screen star Maudie Edwards, aged about eight, with her father Ned and sister, May 1914.

Neath's famous daughter Maudie Edwards already on the road to stardom in 1928.

Maudie Edwards in pantomime as Aladdin, in London, 1940s.

Participants in the Sunday School concert of Siloh Chapel, Melyncrythan, Neath, 1934.

Members of St Catherine's Parish Church, Melyncrythan, Neath, during their nativity performance, Christmas 1941.

Nurses of Neath General Hospital dressed up for a concert in 1941, to entertain World War Two troops.

The young mascot of the Burrows tinplate works band, 1937.

The full company of the reformed Briton Ferry Amateur Operatic Society in its production of *The Pirates of Penzance*, January 1949.

Neath Girls Choir, early 1950s.

Port Talbot's Burrows Tinplate Works Band, with officials, mascot and trophies, in front of the Jersey Beach Hotel, Aberavon Beach, 1937.

A group of employees from Marks and Spencer's Neath store hit the entertainment trail, in the early 1950s.

Youngsters from Wern Chapel, Aberavon, dressed for a performance of *Hansel and Gretel*, at the New Hall, late 1940.

The cast of *Bless The Bride*, staged at the town's Public Hall, by Briton Ferry Amateur Operatic Society, 1952.

These majorettes step out smartly along Victoria Road, Aberavon, during a Port Talbot hospital carnival parade, early 1950s.

Trefelin Secondary School Girls' Choir, Port Talbot, 1959.

Many of Port Talbot's 1960s teenagers will recall dancing to the sounds of this group – Airborne.

Participants in a Christmas concert given by 1st Neath Guides and Greenwoods, at Neath Methodist Church, 1954.

A group of Neath store workers who dressed up and trod the boards in the name of entertainment, 1952.

Members of Cwmavon YWCA during a concert, 1970.

The cast of the pantomime *Aladdin*, staged at St David's Church Hall, Neath, 1956.

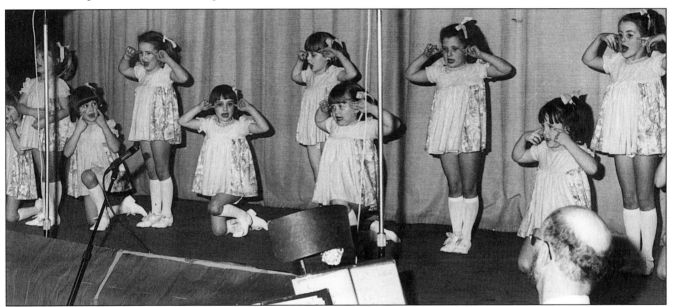

Youngsters from Marlene Boyle's Dance School, during a 1971 production at the Afan Lido, Port Talbot.

Pupils of Alderman Davies Church in Wales Girls' School, Neath, perform the operetta the Feast of St Anne's, 1956.

Pupils of Bryn Primary School, Port Talbot, during a late 1970s Christmas concert.

Members of the Neath Corps of the Salvation Army at a concert in Wesley Chapel, Neath, January 1963.

Team Spirit

Cricket was a serious business for this Neath area team, 1905.

Aberavon-Port Talbot RFC, mid-1920s.

Neath Harlequins with their spoils from a productive 1928-29 season.

Port Talbot's Jack Lewis, Welsh Amateur Boxing Association Champion, 1924.

Competitors in a motorcycle scramble held in fields near Mosshouse Reservoir, Neath, late 1930s.

Vivian Square, Aberavon, quoits team, with a trophy from their successful 1925 season.

Port Talbot Great Western Railway Home Guard darts team, winner of Mr Cunliffe's Cup, 1941.

Orchard Place Baptist Church, Neath, table tennis squad, mid-1930s.

Central School, Port Talbot rugby squad, 1948-49.

Briton Ferry cricket XI, 1932.

The Port Talbot YMCA team who took part in BBC Radio's *Sporting Challenge* quiz 1952.

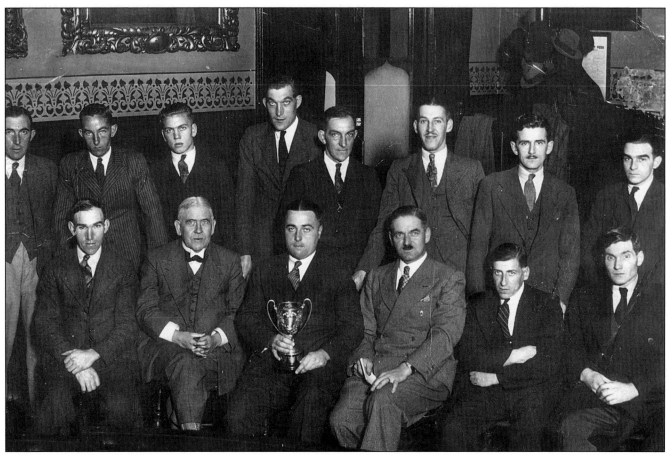

Cimla Cricket Club, winners of the Neath and District Sunday School League, 1934.

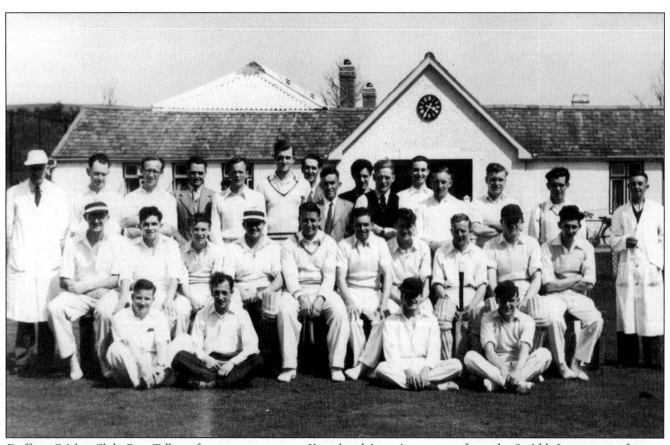

Duffryn Cricket Club, Port Talbot after an away game at Ystradgynlais against a team from the Smith's Instruments factory, sometimes known as the Tick-Tock, 1952.

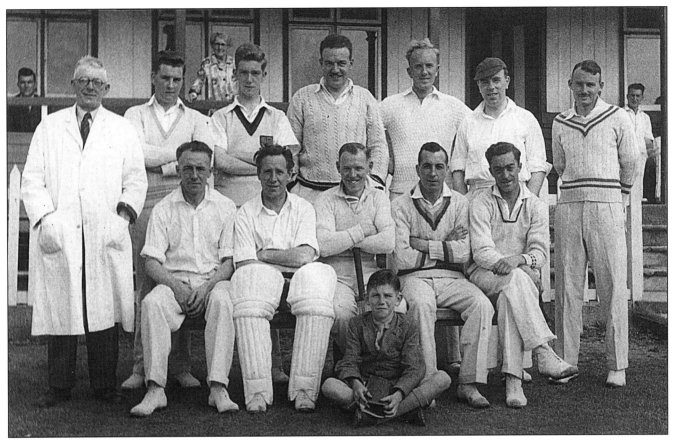

A Briton Ferry Cricket Club team, 1946.

Cwmavon RFC, Port Talbot, at Kenfig Hill, 1954.

Cimla Cricket Club ready for an encounter with a Briton Ferry Steel XI in the early 1950s.

A Trefelin Secondary School, Port Talbot, rugby XV, 1957.

Marks and Spencer staff from Neath all set to board an N&C luxury coach to head off for an inter-store sports day, 1951.

The successful girls athletics squad pictured at Trefelin Secondary School, Port Talbot, 1959.

Cwmavon RFC players, officials, wives and guests at a 1960s presentation evening.

The squad from Marks and Spencer, Neath, which took part in a 1951 inter-store sports day.

Gnoll School netball team, Neath, 1954.

Alderman Davies' Church-
in-Wales School, Neath,
rugby squad 1956-57.

Trefelin Workingmen's
Club, Port Talbot, darts
team, 1963.

Cimla Rugby Club members present president Alderman T E C Molland with a framed picture of himself on his installation as Mayor of Neath, 1962.

Port Talbot athlete Jim O'Brien, captain of the Steel Company of Wales Harriers, receives the team trophy after an inter-club event at the company's Margam sports ground, 1965.

Awards night at Neath Cage Bird Association, 1963.

Trefelin Workingmen's Club darts team, Port Talbot, mid-1960s.

Players, officials and guests of Cimla Cricket Club, Neath, at its Cefn Saeson pavilion, 1964.

A group of five-a-side football teams at Cymmer Afan Youth Wing, Port Talbot, 1966.

Gnoll Junior School seven-a-side rugby team, 1973.

A civic start for a charity football match between a team of players from Bryn AFC, Port Talbot, and a special team of past players from Swansea City AFC, 1970s.

Cimla AFC, Neath, 1974-75.

Goytre Junior Football Club, Port Talbot, 1975.

Cimla AFC, Under-18s team, reigning West Wales Youth Cup winners and champions of division three, Neath and District Soccer League 1978.

Goytre United AFC, Under-11s team, Port Talbot, 1977.

Alderman Davies' Church-in-Wales School, Neath, football team, 1984.

Glanafan Lower School, Port Talbot, rugby team, 1978.

Alderman Davies' Church-in-Wales School, Neath, rugby team, 1984.

Glanafan Lower School, Port Talbot, football team, 1978.

Members of Afan Valley Angling Club, Port Talbot, at the town's civic centre, receiving a grant from the Sports Council for Wales, from the town's mayor, Alderman Graham Jones, 1977.

The start of the first 10K run organised by Aberavon Green Stars RFC, Sandfields, Port Talbot, mid-1980s.